# Rich Kid Poor Kid: The battle for public education

First published in 2026 by Australia Institute Press
Reprinted 2026



ISBN 978-1-7642205-4-5 (paperback with flaps)
ISBN 978-1-7642205-8-3 (paperback)
ISBN 978-1-7642205-5-2 (ebook)

Published in Australia and New Zealand by
Australia Institute Press
www.australiainstitute.org.au



Cataloguing-in-publication data is available from the National Library of Australia

Copyedited by Rod Morrison

Printed and bound in Australia by McPherson's Printing Group, an accredited ISO AS/NZS 14001 Environmental Management Systems printer.

# Rich Kid Poor Kid: The battle for public education

Jane Caro

Australia Institute
⟶ Press

# How did we end up pitting our kids against one another?

When my father was offered a job in Sydney in 1963, my mother was keen to move. That year was one of the grimmest English winters in living memory and while our village of Swanland in Yorkshire was picturesque, it was also knee-deep in snow. Lots of frozen Brits migrated to Australia in 1963, including, I was delighted to discover, Angus and Malcolm Young, who went on to form AC/DC. The lure of sunny Sydney was too much to resist. But my mother had one proviso: she would only take her three children — aged from my two-year-old brother to five-year-old me — to a country where she could send them to the local public school. For her, that was the mark of a truly civilised society.

My mother was born in Manchester in 1931 to a lower-middle-class family in an era when your position in the social hierarchy was rigid and unforgiving. She was very conscious of her Lancashire accent and humble social status. My father came from a somewhat posher middle-class family and had been to Manchester Grammar School and Cambridge University. As he rose through the ranks of the multinational Reckitt and Colman, my mother was painfully aware that every time she opened her mouth, she was instantly defined as "common". Still alive and well at the age of 94, she is a very intelligent woman, but brains didn't matter much for girls with regional working-class accents in 1950s England.

One of the reasons my parents have been happily married for so long — 70 years and counting — is because my mother's brains *did* matter to my dad. He has always said that she is the smartest person he knows. He is right. Both my parents believed strongly in the right of every child to realise their potential, regardless of their position in society. They still believe that.

My mother remembers the sting of being dismissed. Her ingrained sense of inferiority, inculcated by the class anxiety her parents suffered from all their lives — it did not do to get above yourself — thwarted her in many ways. As a result, she has always been passionate about equality and angry about her lack of it. She and my father rose up the ladder economically, but their children were taught that our privilege gave us obligations as well as benefits. Our responsibility was to spread privilege, not clutch it tightly to ourselves and others like us. We have all taken this lesson to heart. The importance of a high-quality public school in every suburb and town, supported by locals, was and is at the heart of my mother's world view.

In 1963, Sydney and most Australian towns and cities easily lived up to her hardly exacting standard. Tragically, there are many people today who feel that such confidence in the quality of their neighbourhood school is no longer a given. Only about 60% of Australian children now attend public schools, with many more attending public primary schools than public secondary ones. Families literally beggar themselves to get their kids into private schools, with high school fees now one of the top five reasons for bankruptcy.[1]

It is in no small part due to my parents' passionate belief in the importance of public education, including my mother's advocacy for DOGS (the National Council for the Defence of Government Schools) back in the day, that I have been an activist for the importance of a strong, well-resourced public education system for more than a quarter of a century. I first got active while pregnant with my first child back in 1988 when people started asking me what private school I had put his/her (her as it turned out) name down for. I was astonished. My children would go to their local public school, as I had done. What on earth were these people thinking? That's when I first became aware that neoliberalism had taken a hatchet to the education system that I had benefited from and taken for granted.

My comprehensive public school cohort in the 1970s included everyone from the Housing Commission kids across the road to the sons and daughters of doctors, architects and CEOs. We didn't know what anyone's father did, nor did we care. At my recent 50-year school reunion — organised by a few of us in our spare time; no well-funded alumni associations for public school grads — I spent a wonderful afternoon and evening with a group of people whose only connection was that we'd all gone to high school together.

My old schoolmates had followed many and varied pathways through life. Some had earnt big bucks, others not so much. Some had lots of children, others none at all. Some were what the wider world would have called "successful", others had navigated more than their fair share of difficulties. Some had spent decades living and working overseas, others had spent all their lives in the suburbs we grew up in. None of it mattered. In our mid-sixties, we seemed a group of more-or-less content, contributing and useful members of Australian society. And we were all grateful for the opportunities our education in a bog-standard NSW public high school had given us, regardless of who our parents were. These are the very schools that we have largely lost, especially in our cities.

What did we change that so undermined these local schools or, at least, our trust in the quality of them? When did so many Australians start to believe that good schools were private and public schools were crap?

When I went to school, between 1963 and 1974, nobody talked about school choice. Almost everyone sent their child to the public school up the road. By high school, those of us at public schools actively pitied the kids whose parents had forced them to attend the private variety. We could wear our hair long and our skirts short as the fashions of the day dictated. Private school boys had to have a short back and sides haircut at the end of every school holiday — I dumped one poor boy because having a short-haired boyfriend was social suicide. Private school girls were subjected to having the length of their hems measured and — this was creepy — regular knicker inspections. We felt superior to our private school peers, and they knew it.

It wasn't just the students who were dismissive of the private offering. My parents and their friends never even discussed it. Fierce arguments raged about the Vietnam War, women's lib and the death penalty, certainly. But the right to choose your kid's school? Not a dickybird. When did that begin to change? When did attending a public school become almost shameful? And what has the plummeting status of the schools open to everyone achieved? That is what this essay sets out to discover, and to do that, I must go back to the 1960s.

—

I believe the rot set in soon after my family migrated to Australia thanks to the actions of a triumvirate of prime ministers: Robert Menzies, Gough Whitlam and Malcolm Fraser. In 1964, the year after we arrived, Menzies began giving federal capital grants to private, fee-charging schools. It was a controversial policy and it inflamed what was known as the "state aid debate", which had ebbed and flowed since the mid-19th century and had been championed by the Democratic Labor Party (DLP) who wanted public subsidies for Catholic schools.

Menzies' 1964 *State Grants (Science Laboratories and Technical Training) Act*[2] was extended in 1970 to give recurrent grants to private, fee-charging schools. Then, in 1974, the Whitlam Labor government extended this funding from the federal government to *all* schools in Australia. Prior to that, public schools were funded entirely by state governments and private schools by the fees paid by the families whose children attended them.

When Malcolm Fraser became prime minister in 1975, the Coalition gave preferential increases in Commonwealth funding to private schools, based on an assumption that public schools were the responsibility of the states. This division has evolved through cumulative political and policy decisions by successive Coalition and Labor governments to the benefit of one system and the detriment of the other.

Like Menzies, who gave capital grants for science and technical education and school libraries, Whitlam argued that recurrent federal funding was educationally necessary. It was the height of the post-war baby boom and schools — particularly Catholic schools — were bursting at the seams. Almost all my classes, as I went through the NSW public school system, contained at least 40 kids. Given the Catholic church's view on contraception, Catholic schools had a particular problem with overcrowding. There was a saying at the time that when someone was drunk, they were "as full as a Catholic school". That's why the Bishop of Goulburn's dramatic closure of all the Catholic schools in his diocese, telling the families whose children attended them to go to the nearby public ones, had such an effect.

He certainly picked his timing.

The Bishop's flourish was temporary, of course,

but it is the foundation of one of the myths used to defend public funding of private schools to this day. Namely that the public system would collapse if we closed private schools. Setting aside that no one is seriously suggesting closing all private schools, in today's Australia, a rapidly falling birth rate has radically changed the situation. Public schools would welcome the overwhelmingly middle-class families that fill today's Catholic (and Anglican and Christian) schools with open arms. They might even kill a fatted calf.

But Whitlam's policy of federally funding all schools was not just about education. It had another benefit. It helped mend the split between the Catholic and conservative DLP and the secular and progressive Australian Labor Party (ALP). It was a split that had kept Labor out of government for 23 long years. Recurrent funding to private, fee-charging schools, most of which then and now are part of the Catholic education system, helped bring Catholic parents and, even more importantly, the Catholic lobby, back into the Labor fold.

There was another reason why recurrent public funding for Catholic schools was so attractive to the church. From a peak in the mid-1960s, the number of young Catholics becoming nuns, brothers and priests began to fall. Nuns, in particular, were becoming harder to attract and retain and it was they who often took on the bulk of teaching.[3] This meant that the Catholic education system had to compete with the public system for teachers and that meant paying them a competitive salary. Costs were rising. It is worth pointing out here that the Catholic church then and now is one of the wealthiest institutions in Australia, currently worth an estimated $25–30 billion.[4] Yet it was to the Australian taxpayer that the church turned when it needed to start paying its teachers properly.

Malcolm Fraser, when he was education minister in the Gorton and McMahon Coalition governments, introduced the neoliberal funding scheme that Australia is now saddled with. When Fraser took charge of our school system, he embedded a "basic grant" for all non-government schools regardless of need. His justification was pure neoliberalism:

> We believe it is the democratic right of persons to be allowed to establish independent schools such as we have

> in Australia. We do not believe in government monopoly … We categorically reject the argument that because a significant number of citizens choose to seek a form of education for their children which they preferred to the state system and are prepared to make financial sacrifices, those citizens cannot expect any help from the state even though they are easing its financial and physical burden.[5]

Over the period of the Fraser government, total Commonwealth funding for schools increased by 27%. Over the same period, funding for public schools decreased by 7%, while funding for private schools almost doubled.[6] This set up a pattern of funding and a set of rationalisations that are followed to this day. These policies began the process of undermining public education.

There was unease about giving public money to private schools. The previously mentioned group DOGS — the National Council for the Defence of Government Schools — was launched in the 1960s specifically to fight the granting of state aid to private — overwhelmingly religious — schools. In 1980, DOGS mounted a High Court challenge claiming the funding contravened Section 116 of the Australian Constitution which states the Commonwealth "shall not make any law for establishing any religion". But in February 1981, six out of seven High Court judges ruled that funding for religious schools was valid because it was for educational purposes and not for "establishing a religion".[7] DOGS had lost their case, and the Australian school landscape shifted inexorably.

—

The right to an education is one of the few rights that is enshrined in law in New South Wales, but schooling can also be seen as a public, a private and a "positional" good. The changes in the way Australia funded its different school sectors began to shift our education system from the public to the positional, from left to right, if you like. It is that snowballing movement, encouraged by various governments over the last half century, which has got us to where we are today. Let's begin by defining what is meant by public, private and positional good when it comes to our schools.

## Schooling is a public good

Everyone benefits from living in a well-educated society. Employers benefit because they can draw on an educated workforce, but it is our democracy that benefits most. As British Liberal MP, Robert Lowe, Viscount Sherbrooke, said in response to the passage of the 1867 Reform Bill which vastly increased the franchise in Britain, "we must educate our masters".[8] The new voters were all "masters" at that time, given the expanded franchise only included men. Nevertheless, Lowe's point was valid and was understood at the time. If we are to give every citizen an equal (or thereabouts) say in the governing of our country, then we must educate them to be able to exercise that vote responsibly.

Free, secular, universal and public education available to every child regardless of the accident of their birth is indivisible from democracy. If democracy is the system of government where every citizen has the same rights as everyone else, then the undermining of public education inevitably also undermines the health of our democracy.

By 1870, the *Elementary Education Act* established a system of primary education for all children in Britain. Australia was a little ahead of what was then considered the "Mother Country". Our first public school was established in 1848. Interestingly, Robert Lowe spent seven years in Sydney during the 1840s. Public schools, open to all regardless of parents or background, were formed primarily to advance the public good.

There is nothing new about private education. It's been around since kings first hired tutors for their sons (rarely their daughters). Public education for every child regardless of background was, and remains, a revolutionary idea. Some conservatives still decry it as "socialism". Yet any tinpot dictatorship can and always has created a highly educated elite. It takes a well-organised civil society to create a well-educated general population which may be why it was such an important symbol for my mother. And the benefits of universal education are quantifiable. Public education is a public good because it increases literacy rates across the population and this has a measurable, positive effect on the wealth and prosperity of the entire nation, whether every citizen personally attended a public school or not.[9]

## Schools are a private good

Schools equip students with the necessary skills to navigate society. To be able to read, write, add, subtract and multiply are point of entry in today's world. Anyone without these basic skills will struggle to make their way. Indeed, literacy rates are one criterion by which we define a developed country. People often feel shamed and excluded if they lack basic literacy and numeracy skills.

While public schools contribute to this private good by offering access to learning to every child, private schools market themselves specifically on the competitive aspect. They exploit an individual's desire to succeed ahead of others. Too much emphasis on private good creates a dog eat dog (or child eat child) view of education. This competition for better marks also feeds parents' increasing fear of what may happen to their children if they get left behind. Private good focuses on the right of an individual to prosper, not the community.

From their inception, which long predates public schools, private schools existed to maintain their religion's power and dominance. Protestant schools wanted to increase literacy so everyone could read the Bible. Eventually, the Catholic church also decided this was a good idea. They weren't always so keen. In 1536, the English scholar William Tyndale was strangled and burnt at the stake for daring to translate the Bible into English.

## Schools as a positional good — as brands

It is as a "positional" good — that is, a product or service in limited supply that consumers want more of as their income increases — that the self-declared "elite" schools come into their own.

Many well-heeled parents (or those in possession of well-heeled grandparents) pay large amounts of money to be associated with particular private schools. Having worked in the advertising industry, I am well-versed in how premium brands depend on charging high prices. High prices are one of the ways these brands create the impression they are superior. We have been groomed for generations to believe that the more you pay for something the better it is. That's why premium brands do not actually have to be worth more, just appear to be. The positional good gained from purchasing a premium brand is the status its possession bestows upon the consumer. Turning left when you board a plane doesn't get you to your destination any quicker, or even more safely. It may get you there in more comfort and even luxury, which is pleasant, but the reason you are getting on a plane in the first place is the same, whatever seat you sit in.

The major selling point of any form of "first class", whether on an airline or for exotic coffee or luxurious quilted toilet paper, is the boost to the purchaser's ego and their sense of their importance or "position" in society. When I see an expensive SUV proudly flaunting a sticker declaring "I'm a (insert name of posh school here) Mum" (such stickers really exist) I know exactly what those parents have bought, and it isn't, necessarily, a better education. It feels more like membership of an exclusive and therefore highly desirable club. Especially as many of these publicly subsidised high-fee schools now offer facilities beyond the dreams of wildest avarice. Consider these random examples: a library built to look like a Scottish castle (exclusive does not equal tasteful); sports stadiums the envy of professional football teams; an air conditioned equestrian centre (can't have the students riding a hot horse); plunge pools for headmasters; and a wellbeing centre featuring no fewer than six ice baths for recovery sessions (getting overheated seems to be a theme) along with a 25-metre pool.

I have often argued that Catholic and other so-called "low" fee schools (low to whom and compared to what?) rely on the glittering brands of high-fee schools like Riverview, Abbotsleigh, Geelong Grammar, Churchie (the Anglican Church Grammar School), PLC, King's, St Paul's, Somerville House, Ascham, Frensham, St Margaret's, Lauriston Girls and so on that make the private school brand so aspirational. These so-called "elite" schools work in the same way that haute couture works for European fashion houses. Few can afford the clothes Dior, Yves Saint Laurent, Dolce & Gabbana, Louis Vuitton or Balenciaga send down the runway. High fashion's unattainability is, in fact, the point. How can anything be exclusive if it does not exclude most people?

It appears to be human nature to yearn most for what is hardest to get. Yet almost everyone can have a taste of such exclusive brands by purchasing their lipstick, skincare products, perfume, or sunglasses. Yes, those items are also ridiculously overpriced, but they are within the reach of the many, not just the few. Indeed, the turnover from such relatively affordable items bearing the magic brand names is how these fashion houses stay solvent. The loss-making but highly publicised haute couture is really just an advertising campaign for the mass-produced, lower-priced items that keep the businesses alive.

So it is with the Riverviews and Abbotsleighs of this world. Most families could not dream of paying their fees, but they can access a little bit of brand "private" by buying their child a place in a more affordable (although still overpriced) Catholic or Christian school. While I am not convinced that education ought to be a positional good at all, I am absolutely certain that taxpayers' money should not be used to help some schools maintain their prestige and elitism.

Inevitably, once the public funding of private schools became entrenched, our schooling system began to shift from an emphasis on the public good towards the private and positional. The Hawke Labor government's education minister John Dawkins was focused on education that produced workers who would enhance Australia's productivity and international economic competitiveness. He saw education as a national positional good. Researchers at Queensland University of Technology have written of the Hawke government's reforms that, "While equity and access were promoted, they were framed in terms of social efficiency, resulting in the individual and the economy being placed centre stage."[10]

## The myth of choice

The Howard Coalition government took Hawke and then Keating's economic rationalist attitude to education and turbocharged it, further shifting the focus from the public and democratic benefit of schooling towards the private and positional. They increased the marketisation of schools and promoted the absurd idea that compulsory education for every child could survive intact in a system where competition and parental choice not only ruled supreme but were directly encouraged with public funding.

Compulsory education and parental choice trying to coexist does not result in an increase in the amount of choice parents have over the school their child attends. Only families with either money or a talented child ever have much choice anyway. What neoliberal, parental choice policies do is give certain schools choice over which children they will or won't educate. Most of the schools with such a choice are private, but in the neoliberal world of winner schools and loser schools, some public schools are able to make choices about who they will educate too. Ask parents in any neighbourhood or town which are the most "desirable" schools and I'll lay money they overwhelmingly pick the same ones. The schools that become "desirable" can then game the system and maintain their place at the top by carefully choosing students who will improve their results and image in the community. This equates to students as marketing assets.

Every year, regular as clockwork, when the NAPLAN results are made public and league tables and school rankings are used to make cheap content and clickbait for anxious parents, certain schools are lauded while others are castigated. The lauded schools claim all sorts of innovations and techniques that have improved their results, such as explicit teaching (do they mean explaining things clearly?), extra reading times, and tutors in the library. What is rarely made explicit in the articles about the results is how the best performing schools tend to educate the children of the better off, the exceptions being those enrolling the highly motivated children of first-generation migrants and refugees. Overwhelmingly, the schools languishing at the bottom have been left to struggle with the children the more fortunate schools don't want.

At the end of 2025, a group of education experts, including academics and teachers' unions, sent an open letter begging News Corp publications to stop publishing the annual league tables that they called "misleading" and "crude".[11] The letter was rejected on the grounds it criticised the News Corp brand. The unconscious irony of such a response by an organisation cynically running rankings that profoundly damage the brand of many schools (not to mention the chances of the vulnerable children they teach) doesn't bear thinking about.

"Choice" has been a justification for increasing funding to private schools for decades. It is a proxy for "price" and has led to the misleading perception that public subsidies have somehow made private education more affordable. Public funding of private supply rarely leads to a reduction in prices. In fact, it often leads to the opposite, as has been the case in Australia. After decades of publicly funding private schools, Australia now has the most expensive high schools in the developed world.[12]

This was eminently predictable. Just have a look at the effects of first homeowners' schemes and childcare subsidies if you don't believe me. It's basic marketing and economics: in capitalism, the market will always charge what the market can bear. If governments decide to subsidise buyers without capping the fees suppliers can charge, as is the case with private school subsidies, then the supplier, quite sensibly, pockets the subsidy and continues to charge the price they choose. This is why after decades of the most generous public subsidies in the OECD, private school fees consistently rise at a rate higher than inflation every year.[13] Keeping prices high is an integral part of the marketing model. To repeat a question I asked earlier: how can you be exclusive unless you have mechanisms such as fees that exclude?

Under John Howard the emphasis in schooling moved to individual achievement, student and school rankings, league tables and performance measures such as standardised testing. After all, how does a government make children more productive? By testing and ranking them as often as possible. Education researchers from Queensland University of Technology claim that the Howard Coalition government education policies recast the notion of disadvantage "from socio economic to the literacy proficiency of the individual".[14] In other words, everything a child got out of a school, or failed to get out of it, was their own fault, or their parents' fault, or their teachers' fault, or all three. It had nothing to do with systemic and generational disadvantage or deliberate political policy.

What this neoliberal, market-driven view of schooling entirely forgets — or conveniently ignores — is that no child is disadvantaged through any of their own doing. I often think that the biggest risk any of us take in life is to be born. None of us has any control over whom we will be born to, or the circumstances into which we will arrive. If you doubt me, just imagine what it might be like to be born a girl in Afghanistan today. Is her circumstance her own fault? Does she deserve to have her potential limited in ways that other children, in other circumstances, could not even imagine? If she lives a miserable, hand-to-mouth life, characterised by poverty and brutality, is this due to her own failure to "pull herself up by her bootstraps"?

We are all subject to the lottery of birth. Some of us become card-carrying members of the lucky sperm club but most of us do not. My point is this: the circumstances of our birth make a huge difference to the kind of life trajectory we can expect. Yes, there are exceptions, but they are the exceptions that prove the rule. Parents know this, whether they are prepared to admit it or not, when they climb over one another to get their kid into the designated "desirable" school.

Like Margaret Thatcher in Britain and Ronald Reagan in the United States, John Howard lauded those he called "aspirational voters". A mythical group of morally upstanding people who reached for a better life. I suspect we all aspire to a better life. It's just that some of us are better equipped to pursue it. This judgemental view of people — the good ones aspire to get ahead while the bad ones bludge — was behind Howard and his education minister David Kemp's decision to place parental choice at the centre of Australia's education system. This is an expression of the classic neoliberal idea that individuals know what is good for them and therefore the government should get out of the way. What happens after that depends on whether you have made a good choice.

Sounds reasonable, perhaps, but it fails to understand the very different barriers people face as they attempt to make their way in the world (for example, racism, ableism, sexism, homophobia, ageism, poverty and social class). Deliberately creating differential educational opportunities for children based on their parentage via political policy creates a lifelong vicious cycle that locks large numbers of people into limited and difficult lives. We lock them in, then we punish and shame them for being locked in. Neat. Demonising dole bludgers, single mothers, immigrants or welfare cheats is an easy kick. Worse, this lazy demonising gives governments permission to use education funding to reward the parents the government sees as "good" and punish the parents the government sees as "bad".

Aspiration, in the Howard universe, is about social advancement — getting ahead of others.

It is a positional good, in other words, and fundamentally opposed to equality of opportunity. What's the best way to ensure you and yours get ahead? Hobble those you regard as your competitors. It is a truism that those most in favour of any competition are always those most likely to win it.

## Meddling and moralising in public schools

The Howard government's white anting of the public education system was not just a matter of funding. Howard was the prime minister who famously declared that public education was "politically correct" and "values neutral".[15] This was startling, because public education is the only schooling system that accepts every child regardless of their background. It is also the only schooling system that places public good at its centre. I find it hard to think of a more admirable moral value than embracing all children and doing everything you can to help them learn.

However, not content with the insult, Howard added injury by mandating a series of patronising demands aimed at injecting supposedly missing morals back into classrooms. To that end the government sent a poster to every school, both public and private, featuring an image from World War I: a picture of Simpson and his donkey with a list of nine rather vapid values schools apparently lacked and needed politicians to teach them.[16] The poster was accompanied by threats. Failure to mount it in a prominent place could result in loss of school funding. It seems bullying was a value approved of by the government. I know at least one public school principal who hung the poster as required but immediately turned its face to the wall. I love the bedrock anti-hypocrisy of public schools. Is that a moral value, I wonder?

Howard also insisted that schools run a workshop about the nine values enshrined on his daggy poster. I benefited directly from that imposition. As a professional facilitator I was asked by one public high school to run a workshop. I think that was also a small act of subversion by the school involved. It was held one evening in the school library in a western suburb of Sydney. It went rather well, although not, perhaps, in the way the government intended.

I particularly enjoyed watching a ferociously articulate and intelligent Year 12 student skewer the local MP (a member of Howard's cabinet) who arrived very late, rushing in when the workshop was half over. When she finally settled, the student asked her a series of pointed questions about the hypocrisy of the government's attitudes to public schools and the moral values of fairness, understanding, tolerance and inclusion (all on the poster). Then he added a question about the government-approved value of "respect" and how courtesy and punctuality might play a role. The poor MP was left a gabbling mess. I was left feeling comforted that public schools were still doing what they are designed to do in a democracy — educate students to think critically, especially about those in power.

Many might see Howard's pompous moralising as trivial. Unfortunately, I think it did real damage, particularly to the secular nature of public education. Howard's finger wagging implied that the federal government no longer wholeheartedly supported its public schools or had any interest in the degree of difficulty involved in trying to provide equality of opportunity in an increasingly hostile environment. It also showed the desire of the government to insert its culture wars into schools along with the rest of the public sphere. Worst of all, teachers being told that the schools they worked in, the lessons they taught and the care they offered their students was "values neutral" by their prime minister was a hefty blow to their morale. If you can think of something that would damage the ability of kids to learn more profoundly than lowering the morale of their teachers, I'd like to hear about it.

By openly disapproving of secular schools, Howard gave overt permission for parents to desert the public system which was — according to him — morally inferior. He then made it easier for them to do just that. The Howard government maintained the tradition of giving the wealthiest private schools additional millions every year which they did not need to apply for. At the same time, via a small set of targeted programs, the neediest communities had to jump through hoops for smaller grants from a limited pool of funds for a fixed period. They had to set up committees of teachers and parents to invest time making submissions, and then meet complex accountability requirements.

Similarly complex requirements were instituted for funding for Indigenous students, but not for the recurrent grants to the wealthy private schools. How could there be, when there was no explicit educational purpose to justify those funds in the first place? Howard's Socio Economic Status (SES) funding scheme shifted assessment of need from resources of the school to measuring parental socio-economic status via their postcode linked to ABS data.[17] His scheme applied only to private schools. A needs-based funding scheme that is only for fee-charging schools is the educational equivalent of a hunger relief program for the well-fed.

In keeping with the moral crusade that characterised Howard's interventions in education, his government also instituted something called the National School Chaplaincy Program.[18] This was a further insult to the inclusive nature of public education. Public schools, funded by every taxpayer and open to every taxpayer's child must, in my opinion, be secular. If they give primacy to one religion over another and indeed over no religion, then they become correspondingly less welcoming and less inclusive.

Sold to the public as a way to help children in public schools escape their valueless teachers (did they really mean Godless?), chaplains were meant to provide pastoral care and welfare to students but, we were told, they would not proselytise. This left an obvious logic gap: if they would not preach their gospel, why did chaplains need to be religious at all?

Like the SES system itself, the justifications for school chaplaincy have always sounded hollow. Despite the rules loosening from time to time, state governments continue to outsource the provision of the program — worth over $60 million per annum — to third-party providers who are overwhelmingly Christian. The clue, after all, is in the name. Most chaplains have ties to Christian churches, are trained in theology, or are ordained. The National School Chaplaincy Program is a direct assault on the inclusive, secular values of public schools and increases the perception that public schools are moral deserts in need of guidance by a nicer class of preacher. It also feeds the insidious notion that public schools are unsafe.

No doubt some school chaplains do a good job, but it is also true that the need for properly qualified, well-trained school counsellors, psychologists, social workers and specialist learning support staff has only continued to grow, especially in the very schools with rapidly increasing concentrations of needy kids. Chaplains, fuelled by a mission from God, are cheaper than other trained professionals. But is saving souls for Jesus the role of secular public education? I wonder how the parents of Muslim, Hindu, Jewish, Zoroastrian and atheist kids see it? And well-meaning as most chaplains may be, kids with high needs require support from professionals with high skills. Send the chaplains to the religious private schools. Any public school parent who wants religious instruction for their children, and many do, can send them to their religion's equivalent of Sunday School.

In New South Wales, public schools must set aside one hour a week for religious instruction, often called scripture. Children may opt out, but they are not allowed to do much of anything else during that time. Ethics classes, often supervised by parents annoyed by this religious constraint, are run in some schools as an alternative. I think the chaplaincy program, like so much else the God-fearing, free marketers have imposed on public education, had many motivations. Not least the desire to appear to be doing good, but on the cheap.

## The high price of vouchers

Prior to 1996, under the Hawke government's New Schools Policy, if you wanted to open a new private school and receive public funding you had to demonstrate the need based on population.[19] You also had to prove that the new school would not cannibalise any other publicly funded schools already operating in the area.

John Howard got rid of such anti-competitive rubbish. "Red tape", he would have called it. Instead, new fee-charging schools were provided with establishment grants and given carte blanche to service already over-serviced areas. Private schools, due to the fees they charge, are most interested in opening schools in areas where they calculate parents can pay. Better off parents were cast as consumers in an education market who could choose which schools they would pay for. Those children without such parents were cast to the wolves. This was when the education hunger games really began.

Instead of an education system working to provide equal learning opportunities for all, we now had an education market where, as is true in all markets, the better resourced had the most chance of corralling opportunities for themselves. Many middle-class parents now appear to view public schools as a welfare system of last resort for the children of the poor.

The now notorious American theocratic organisation, the Heritage Foundation, has a chapter on education in its 900-page manifesto, *Mandate for Leadership*, often called Project 2025.[20] In essence, it recommends President Trump implement a similar education system in the United States to the one John Howard saddled Australia with a quarter of a century ago. The main difference is that in our system the funding "voucher" per student goes to the school. In the United States it will go to the parent.

The neoliberal voucher system for funding education has had the same result wherever it has been implemented. Vouchers accelerate inequality and decimate the educational opportunities of the children born with the least, because better off parents can add money to the voucher, while poorer children's parents can't. Pinochet's Chile (yes, an actual fascist regime) introduced vouchers in 1981, creating the kind of polarised schooling system we now have in Australia. So negative were the effects, in the decades since, Chile has undertaken major reforms, walking back its market-based system.[21] Despite this, Chile still has some of the most expensive schools in the OECD. Not coincidentally, so do we.

What educational vouchers fail to acknowledge is that children are not widgets. They are not all the same and they do not cost the same to educate. Indeed, the ability to create economies of scale between urban, middle-class kids who are generally cheaper to educate, and remote and regional kids from poorer families who are generally more expensive to educate, is one of the great strengths of public education systems that enrol the majority of children. Given that, it is infuriating that we have a system which invests public money in helping the middle class abandon public schools, thus reducing the efficiency and effectiveness of the system as a whole. Schooling in Australia operates in a way that increases the value of the voucher in the private system, since they cream off the least costly to educate students, leaving them with a "profit" which can be spent on fancy buildings and marketing, but with little evidence of improved results. In the public system, the cost of educating students increases while the value of their funding decreases.

Public schools, due to their responsibility for universal, compulsory education, must be kept open in areas where they enrol uneconomically low numbers of students. What's more, when you remove the majority of the cheaper and easier to educate students (aka the middle class) you increase concentrations of disadvantage, thereby increasing the per-student cost, and diluting economies of scale. This further reduces the efficiency and effectiveness of the public system, while also emphasising its necessity.

The system as a whole is geared to producing concentrations of poverty in public schools, amplifying and compounding student disadvantage. The continuing decline in results, as measured by international comparisons, is grim evidence that if there are any gains in concentrating advantage, they are far outweighed by the losses that are caused by concentrations of disadvantage.

## Missed opportunities

The next major development in Australian schooling happened under the auspices of the Rudd, then Gillard, Labor governments. There was finally an attempt at meaningful reform, mainly because all this neoliberal, pseudo market-based education zealotry had not improved results. Education experts were getting itchy about our performance internationally. Shock jocks were too, although their reasons as to why it had happened (lousy teachers) and how to fix it (fire lousy teachers) created more of the very problems they claimed to be trying to fix. Teachers' unions — particularly those with members who were struggling at the coalface of underfunded schools — as well as some state governments, both Labor and Coalition, also started to agitate.

Commissioned by Kevin Rudd in 2010 and published the following year, the Gonski review summarised the sorry state of our schools after decades of neoliberal reforms, revealing that student performance had declined at all levels over the previous decade.[22] By 2009, Australia was in seventh place for literacy, down from second in 1999; and 13th place for maths, down from third.[23] The report also highlighted growing inequality and polarisation and made recommendations aimed at improving equity, particularly around funding reform and how need could be defined. A popular public campaign to have the report recommendations implemented was launched by the public education sector with the slogan "Give a Gonski". It worked. Most ordinary Australians, wherever they sent their kids, were in favour of giving a Gonski.[24]

When she was education minister in the Rudd government, Julia Gillard said that postcode should not dictate destiny. A fine sentiment, but when she became prime minister in June 2010, she carried on with the kind of market-driven, neoliberal education policies that entrench postcode-style generational privilege and underprivilege.

Gillard committed to a new funding model with the express aim of catapulting Australia into the world's top five education systems by 2025.[25] Sadly, by 2018, we sat at 16th in reading, 17th in science and 29th in maths. Things had improved somewhat by 2022, mostly, according to experts, because other countries had fallen back. Nevertheless, since PISA testing began in 2000, we have declined by 37 points in maths, 20 points in science and 30 points in reading.[26]

While they may not give it much thought, I doubt most parents who send their kids to private schools want to actively undermine the education of those less fortunate. I hope not, anyway. The "Give a Gonski" campaign was aimed at making sure the new prime minister took action. When it was first released, not just the public, but all school sectors supported its approach. This was a highly unusual and, as it turned out, fragile coalition. Had Gillard acted quickly, Australia's education system might be in a very different place right now. Unfortunately, she dragged her heels.

Even before the report was released, she announced that no school would lose a dollar.[27] This turned out to be disastrous. It was in direct opposition to the School Resource Standard (SRS) recommendation that school funding be calculated according to the minimum number of resources each school needed to do its job. Some schools desperately needed more resources to support the expensive to educate (aka disadvantaged) students they disproportionately enrolled, while other schools already received more — in some cases far more — than they needed to educate the more fortunate children sitting in their classrooms.

What happened when Gillard refused to change the funding criteria for private schools was the Gonski reforms became much more expensive than they would have been and the wheels began to wobble. The private school lobby saw its opportunity. What had started out as "sector-blind, needs-based" education reforms soon turned into the "sector-based, needs-blind" model of old. It was at this point that we began to hear schools described as over- or underfunded according to their SRS. As I write this, 14 long years since the Gonski review, according to SRS all public schools, bar a handful in the Australian Capital Territory, are underfunded; while all private schools, bar a handful in the Northern Territory, are overfunded.[28]

But back to 2011. Gillard continued to delay the implementation of the review's recommendations, despite the vociferous support of some surprising champions, including the Coalition education minister in New South Wales, Adrian Piccoli, and the premier, Barry O'Farrell. Their support, which was far more enthusiastic than Gillard's, was crucial, because they crossed the political divide. Gillard finally legislated the already compromised Gonski reforms as part of the *Australian Education Act* on 27 June 2013. Gillard lost the prime ministership on the same day to her old foe and previous prime minister,

Kevin Rudd. Labor was trying to hang on to the deckchairs. It didn't work. In September 2013, Rudd lost government to Tony Abbott and the Coalition returned to power.

Abbott's prime ministership only lasted for two turbulent years, which was a relief to many, but especially to the public school community. After famously promising that there would be no cuts to health, education or the ABC if he won the election, Abbott's first budget attempted to cut them all. There was an outcry, and his pre-election promise was used to force him to moderate his cuts. Nonetheless, although the figure is disputed due to complicated accounting considerations, including committing to only part of the projected Gonski increases, Abbott cut up to $30 billion from schools.[29] After breaking such a promise, eating a raw onion — skin and all — and deciding to knight the Duke of Edinburgh, Abbott lost the support of Australians and his party.

It was the beginning of a revolving door of Coalition prime ministers. Abbott was replaced by Malcolm Turnbull who declared that he intended to end the "school funding wars" but, if anything, he carved them in stone. By this time, the funding decisions made by various governments, both federal and state, meant that the Commonwealth (a name carrying considerable irony from the perspective of public schools) was now supposed to be providing around 20% of the funding to public schools from its education budget, leaving 80% to be provided by the states from theirs. The reverse was true for private schools, who received 80% federally and about 20% from the states.

These percentages were the haphazard outcome of decades of compromises, not some kind of holy writ, but Turnbull decided to enshrine them in formal legislation. This was not a recommendation of the Gonski review, although Turnbull wheeled out David Gonski, the chair of the review, to support his announcement. Public school supporters warned that this would be disastrous, as it has turned out. Turnbull's funding scheme turned the Gonski review on its head. After all, if you legislate the division of funding based entirely on the sector a school belongs to and ignore the needs of its students, how can it be anything but sector-based and needs-blind?

Turnbull's legislation cemented the illogical and unfair system whereby the tier of government with the major revenue-raising powers funded the system with the lowest share of children with actual needs, leaving the public system to depend on the states, who bear the burden of delivering services. The technical term for this problem is VFI, Vertical Fiscal Imbalance, which sounds like something that needs treating with noxious dietary supplements.

## Not so common wealth

The Commonwealth's funding contribution to schools — now totalling approximately $33 billion — is carved up unequally between the private and public sectors, with private schools receiving around 62% of the total.[30] The difference is even more stark when you consider that there are around twice as many students in the public system as there are in the private system. Giving more money to the already well-resourced in the name of "fairness" has become the Australian way. The game is rigged. Whether heads or tails, private schools win.

Tasmania and the Northern Territory are our poorest jurisdictions and both are poor for the same reason: more of their taxpayers are from the lowest income households than elsewhere, which means their governments gather less in tax, making it harder to adequately fund services. The fact that more of their residents are on low incomes also means their needs are greater, but their funding pool is smaller. Tasmania and the Northern Territory have even more expensive to teach kids concentrated in disadvantaged schools than other states, but they cannot, on their own, raise the revenue they need to adequately help.

Nice, neat, bureaucratically approved equations don't work for real human children. Indigenous students living in remote parts of the Northern Territory are among the most expensive to educate in Australia, given the costs of services in remote locations. They cost far more than the nice, mostly white, middle-class kids living in Melbourne or Sydney, who, if they attend private schools, receive from both the public and private purse vastly more than they need. Whenever I hear someone arguing that we've "thrown" money at education and seen little improvement in return, I always point out it's because we've been "throwing" it at the wrong kids.

Our funding system, on every level, is completely arse about, if our aim is to offer every child the chance to realise their potential. Mind you, as I hope I have convinced you by now, we seem to be confused about what our education system is for. We make all sorts of motherhood statements about fairness and equality of opportunity, realising every child's potential and the public good purposes of schooling when education ministers hold their annual gathering, but we make precisely no effort to live up to them.

This leads me to ask the following questions about what our schooling system is designed to do. Is it to create a class system? If so, it has been very successful. Is it to reward the parents governments approve of and punish those they disapprove of? If so, job well done. Is it to entrench the power and privilege of the church, organisations which appear to be losing power and privilege everywhere else? If it is, that's been achieved beyond even the most devout believer's fervent prayers. Is it to insulate the children of the anxious middle class from any of their less fortunate peers? Again, bravo. Is it to educate an elite who will run the country, as their fathers and grandfathers have done, and maintain their privilege? Go to the top of the class.

Sorry to sound so cynical, but I've been watching what we are doing in education for a while and I'm not sure how it is possible to be anything else. The purpose of our education system certainly does not seem to be about rewarding merit wherever it emerges and encouraging excellence in every child. You simply cannot achieve that if you give differential educational opportunities to kids based solely on the accident of their birth.

But more about that later. No potted history of the damage done to public schools would be complete without mentioning Scott Morrison's term as prime minister. Morrison made no secret of his preference for private schools. As a Pentecostal Christian he sent his daughters to a religious private school, as have every one of the prime ministers I've mentioned, bar Anthony Albanese and Julia Gillard. Albo sent his son to NSW public schools from kindergarten to Year 12, despite (or perhaps because of) being himself a graduate of the Catholic system. Julia Gillard does not have any children.

Morrison took John Howard's infamous "values neutral" remark even further. In an interview with ex-private school teacher turned shock jock, Alan Jones, Morrison claimed that a Victorian high school program designed to reduce family violence which included role plays dealing with teens struggling with their sexuality made his "skin curl". Did he mean crawl? Or toes curl?[31] No matter, the public got the gist. The culture war misinformation about what is taught in public schools got spread a little wider, further undermining confidence in the system.

Morrison went on to say:

> I don't want the values of others being imposed on my children in my school and I don't think that should be happening in public or private schools. That's why I want to protect the independent schools to ensure they can continue on providing at least that choice. When it comes to public schools … how about we just have state schools that focus on things like learning maths … learning science.[32]

Morrison seemed to be unaware that public schools teach the same curriculum as private schools, apart from a small number of high-fee schools that offer the Baccalaureate in place of other state-based final year assessments. If one system concentrates on teaching maths, so does the other. As for imposing "the values of others", public schools are the only schools that can guarantee they only teach evidence-based science in science classes, without their fingers crossed behind their back. Nor will they ever fire a teacher or any other staff member because they have remarried after divorce, become pregnant out of wedlock, or have a same-sex partner.

Morrison's disdain for secular public schools and his religious zealotry go a long way to explaining why he was so generous with extra money to already overfunded private schools and so parsimonious towards underfunded public ones. Not that anyone in the public school sector was surprised. When he confounded the pundits by winning the 2019 federal election, I was at a wedding. As the results came in there was a lot of surreptitious scrolling among the guests. When it became clear that Labor leader Bill Shorten had lost and Scott Morrison had squeaked home by two seats, one of the guests burst into tears. She was the principal of a secondary public school servicing one of the most disadvantaged cohorts of students in New South Wales. Her distress was so profound she had to leave the wedding. She knew exactly what her students could expect from the new PM. Absolutely nothing.

She was sadly correct. Morrison literally threw money — around $10 billion — at private schools using Gonski and COVID-19 as a cover. The Morrison government's JobKeeper scheme was intended to support businesses that might otherwise have been forced to lay off staff due to the pandemic. He extended the scheme to include wealthy private schools and even allowed private universities like Notre Dame to collect JobKeeper, but not public ones.[33] At the height of the COVID-19 pandemic, this amounted to around $750 million in extra funding for private schools.[34] This was despite those schools continuing to receive their recurrent Commonwealth and state grants, which were more than enough to pay their staff. Not to mention school fees, most of which parents continued to pay.

Public schools were given little, even to deal with a brand-new disease. NSW schools had some additional funding for "enhanced cleaning" and received a supply of sanitisers, soap and toilet paper. As I wrote in 2020, one public school teacher told me that their personal protective equipment amounted to "nine rain ponchos, six bars of soap, three tiny bars of hotel soap and 20 rolls of toilet paper — for a school of 900 students".[35] Later in the pandemic when HEPA filters were being recommended for classrooms, public schools were told to "open their windows".[36]

During the pandemic, public schools were never closed. While face-to-face teaching was limited for various periods, a skeleton staff remained on site for the children of essential workers, and the rest of the teachers taught their students remotely. For those students with no access to the internet who could not participate in online learning, governments, both state and federal, did little. NBN Co provided $50 million to phone and internet providers to support kids in low income families, but many disadvantaged schools resorted to printed work sheet packages and phone support.[37]

I am on the board of a charity — the Public Education Foundation — and our small staff moved mountains to get laptops to students who needed them, thanks to sponsorship, donations and a lot of hard work. They drove around personally delivering the hardware. This is laudable but no child in a country as prosperous as Australia should have to rely on charity to get the resources they need to participate in education — even in a pandemic.

The inadequacy of the help that was offered to public schools during this period was derisory. Schools, teachers, parents and students received the message loud and clear: the education of children at public schools, their physical, mental and emotional health was not worth spending money on. The hypocrisy of right-wing pundits and leaders, including the prime minister, when they wanted to reopen the economy and so started wringing their hands over the mental health of disadvantaged kids and the possibility of them being left behind (say what? they'd never shown any concern about either before) as a reason to get teachers and kids back into classrooms and workers back in the office was nauseating.

Australians recognised that Morrison's leadership during the pandemic and during the catastrophic fires that devastated the East Coast of Australia the year before was woefully inadequate. Voters made their displeasure plain at the ballot box in 2022 when the Labor Party led by Anthony Albanese beat the Coalition. I'd love to claim that the Coalition throwing public education under the bus during the pandemic had a decisive impact on that result, but apart from ensuring that teachers turned out in droves to support Labor at polling booths, I suspect it did not.

However, Morrison's unpopularity cannot have been the only reason Australian voters turned away from the party that had been in charge for a decade. Because in 2025, Albanese confounded global trends towards right-wing populism and made Australian electoral history by securing an emphatic victory. He is the first sitting PM to win a second election in two decades. He is also the first PM to try to do something practical to rebalance our appallingly lopsided schools funding system since Menzies first sent public money to private schools in 1964. One of the first things his government did was admit we might have a problem.

The 2023 *Improving Outcomes for All* report, commissioned by federal education minister Jason Clare, contains a pair of statistics that are shocking in their synchronicity.[38] The report showed that 28.9% of public schools are considered disadvantaged, which simply means most of the kids those schools teach come from homes in the lowest socio-economic quartile. At the other end of the spectrum, 28.9% of private schools teach those who come from the highest socio-economic quartile. The same report contains OECD data which warns Australia that we not only have increasing concentrations of disadvantaged children in disadvantaged schools, but that those concentrations are increasing at a faster rate than in almost any other country, only behind Czechia.[39] We're now winning the silver medal for increasing inequality between our children. If we keep at it, we'll probably nab the gold.

As I have mentioned, the only way the most disadvantaged children in our two poorest jurisdictions can get the funding they need is from the federal government. Malcolm Turnbull tried to legislate that possibility away. His solution did not last long. Between May 2024 and March 2025 the Albanese government countered its effect by amending the Act to make Turnbull's 20% funding for public schools a floor, rather than a ceiling. The legislation now specifies that in all states and the Australian Capital Territory the Commonwealth share for public schools must be a minimum of 20%. In the Northern Territory, the share must be a minimum of 40%.

This change is designed to protect the share of funding public schools are entitled to from going backwards. In March 2025, Federal Education Minister Jason Clare announced a funding deal to lift the Commonwealth's funding share for every public school from 20 to a new floor of 25%.

But before you break out the champagne, the old ideas about the right way to subsidise opportunities for rich kids versus poor kids remain. No public school in Australia that is currently below its SRS will be fully funded under Albo's deals until 2034. That's when the bright, shiny kindergartners of 2026 are in Year 8. And, as education economist Adam Rorris points out, accounting tricks mean the states often don't give their public schools the full 80% they are entitled to. These same tricks are not used to calculate the private schools' 20%. See what I mean about the game being rigged?[40] Even worse, public schools will have to jump through performance and compliance hoops before they can get their money. What do private schools have to do in return for theirs? Nothing. Nada. Zip. Just teach the curriculum and obey the law.

# Where is Australian education right now?

What Australia has done over the last half century is create two parallel, publicly funded education systems: one with all the rights, and one with all the responsibilities.

Private schools can be public when it comes to the handing out of public money, but private when it comes to everything else. They can charge any fees they choose. They can open schools wherever they like and refuse to open, or decide to close schools, whenever they like. They can hire and fire whomever they like because they have a statutory exemption from the *Anti-Discrimination Act* and fight hard not only to hang onto it but to extend it via religious freedom bills. They can refuse to enrol and choose to expel whomever they like — or more pertinently — don't like. They can also, if they want to, teach creationism in science classes including the bizarre claim that vegetarian dinosaurs were included on Noah's Ark.[41]

The rationalisations for all this generosity towards non-government schools have remained more or less the same since parental choice became the main driver behind education policy. They remain tied to the classic neoliberal idea, articulated by Malcolm Fraser in the 1970s, that parents have a right to choose the school their children attend, and the state should subsidise them to do just that. The glaringly obvious problem with this justification is that, when a large part of that choice involves fee-charging schools, only parents with money have choice.

The reason public education was first developed was because most families, most of the time, could not afford the actual cost of educating a child — let alone more than one — over 13 years of schooling. Prior to universal, compulsory, secular education, provided free of charge to the end user by the state, most children received rudimentary schooling at best. As I have mentioned, there is nothing new about private education; it is universal *public* education that is the revolutionary idea. Neoliberals justify funding private schools by arguing it expands choice by lowering fees but, as we are about to see, that's an argument you can drive an entire convoy of elaborately decorated private school buses through.

For starters, despite the competition created by parental-choice-driven policies, private school fees have not fallen and have not become more affordable. This is partly due to the effectiveness of fees as a sorting mechanism. If you want to keep the riff-raff out of your school, charging fees they can't afford is a very efficient way to do it. As I mentioned, the public subsidy of private supply is almost always inflationary, unless you cap the prices the private supplier can charge. The refusal to do this by successive governments is one of the reasons so many private schools are now so luxuriously resourced.

What the public funding of private schools — especially high-fee, so-called "elite" schools — has achieved is a publicly subsidised education arms race where such schools must compete against each other to offer ever more extravagant facilities so they can attract the relatively small number of families who can afford their fees. Tragically, their so-called prestige also tempts other families who can ill afford such schools. These self-declared elite schools compete against one another using public subsidies combined with private fees to buy market share. This is not an appropriate use of government education funding. The very fact I need to say that is scarifying.

It bears repeating that far from giving most parents choice, what the policy settings do is give some schools — mostly private, but some public — choice over which kids they will or will not educate. This allows them to maintain their place at the top of the desirability tree. And the most desirable students are overwhelmingly those from higher socio-economic backgrounds with high levels of social capital. Dr Sunil Badami, an academic, public school parent and advocate, has called this the "wealthification" of schools.[42]

The schools themselves are very aware of the competition they are waging. Recently we have watched some of the boater-wearing boys' schools decide to go co-ed. This has led to some fierce opposition from old boys, including ageing alumni weeping public tears about the very idea of girls entering the hallowed halls of their alma mater (oh the irony). Like the ageing alumni, I have also wondered what was behind this sudden attraction to girls. Could these schools have had an epiphany about feminism and the importance to gender equality of girls and boys getting to know one another as people? Or had their enrolments begun to drop?

Such is the illogicality of parents, girls' schools are seen as better for girls (the actual evidence for this is equivocal) but co-ed schools are believed to be better for boys.[43] Of course, one must be at the cost of the other. Nevertheless, this idea may have led to a drop in enrolments in boys' schools. Or as is more likely, have some of the lower fee Catholic and Christian schools begun to eat the high fee GPS schools' lunch, especially as times get tougher and bankruptcy proceedings become more frequent?[44]

There's another possibility. While enrolments in public education have generally fallen to an all-time low, especially in secondary schools, many public schools in wealthier suburbs are bucking this trend. Forget out-of-area enrolments, Cammeraygal High School on Sydney's lower North Shore risks closing its doors to students because it is so over-subscribed.[45] Other so-called "desirable" public schools in New South Wales include Rouse Hill Public, Carlingford West, The

Ponds High, St Ives High and Riverbank Public, all of whom are exceeding their enrolment caps by 600 students or more.[46] Other popular public schools include Cherrybrook Technology High School, Killara High School and Chatswood High School in Sydney; Glenunga International High School in Adelaide; Maryborough High School in Queensland; and Melbourne High School in Victoria.

Have middle-class parents worked out that it is not the ownership of a school that makes the difference but the cohort of kids it is able to enrol? Global research has confirmed repeatedly that the social class of a child's family is the biggest single predictor of success at school.[47] The higher the socio-economic background of a child's family, the better the kid is likely to do. There are all sorts of reasons for this, including the capacity to pay for tutoring, which I shall tackle later in this essay.

So, have the expensive boys' schools been forced to seek students, not just further afield (see all those elaborately decorated private school buses trundling through our suburbs morning and afternoon), but of a different gender to maintain their enrolments? Or are girls popular because they do better at school? A school's position on the annual league tables so beloved by the media and so hated by educators makes a huge difference to their pulling power. Are the boys' schools seeking to enhance their academic reputations by enrolling high-achieving girls? I don't know the answer. Maybe it's all the above.

However, it might be wise to exercise a little caution before enrolling your daughters in any of these pricy religious schools that are suddenly touting for girls. According to a 2024 pilot study by Barcley Consulting into schools on Queensland's Gold Coast, gender equity is highest in public, secular schools and lowest in private, religious ones.[48] The pilot has been considered so successful, a study of 1000 schools is planned for the near future.

Almost every school will have experienced the out-of-the-box cohort which, for no reason anyone can find, is performing well. Same teachers, same curriculum, same school, just different kids. Was it something in the water when they were conceived? Who knows, but as their results send their school rocketing up the annual league tables, so nearby parents start booking in for Open Days. This is how league tables become self-fulfilling prophecies. If a school is seen as "good" (code for high-achieving) more parents will want their children to attend, and burgeoning waiting lists then allow the school to pick and choose whom they will take. Unsurprisingly, they tend to choose the kids who will give the school the best return (aka high results) for the least effort (aka urban, middle class). This is easier for private schools that have no responsibility for in-area enrolments but, as one retired public school principal told me, very little gets between a principal and a high-achieving potential student.

This is all well and good, until you look at the flip side of the equation. As the sought-after schools enrol the more high-achieving students — both public and private — so the children who are not seen as desirable are left out. Left out? Kept out is more accurate. This leads to them also being clustered together. This is why school choice invariably leads to the increasing concentrations of advantaged and disadvantaged kids in advantaged and disadvantaged schools the OECD keeps warning us about.

If a family has money, or can persuade grandparents to part with some, they can buy their kids into a private school. Parents can also try to move into the catchment of a popular public school, either by renting or buying. The stories the principals of such schools tell of parents falsifying addresses and lying about where they live to gain a place would be funny, if they weren't so sad. Similar stories are told about parents suddenly experiencing a religious conversion when they want to send their child to a private religious school.

People who can afford to move and buy into the catchment of desirable public schools are, perhaps, the canniest. As any real estate agent will tell you, living in the catchment of a public primary and, particularly, secondary school with an excellent reputation increases the value of your home, and your residence is the most tax effective investment in Australia. The same is not true of private or selective schools, not even the ritziest, because private school enrolments are not zoned, and selective schools draw from a very wide area. Talk about a positional good — literally.

These days, to get your kid into a desirable school, you need to have a superstar kid or money. It doesn't matter where you live, if you can pay the fees — or pass the scholarship exam —

you're in. This may be why the stress around the cheap route to a prestigious education (what people really mean when they say "good" in my opinion) can lead to headlines such as the ones we saw recently in Sydney about the riot squad being called to the sites of selective school tests. The chaos was so intense around the thousands of highly stressed children sitting for the exams — and their equally anxious parents — staff literally called in the big guns.[49]

A staff member, quoted in the *Sydney Morning Herald*, said, "We were dealing with kids who were freaking out and totally traumatised by what was going on. You could not make up a worse nightmare than what we went through that day."[50] The owner of a tutoring company quoted in the same article spoke about the pressure and competition that now exists around getting a child into the supposedly "right" school. "For some parents, this (test) is as (sic) equally important as the HSC." He went on to say that some parents saw the testing bungle as an opportunity for their child to squeeze in a couple of weeks' more study. "That's how cut-throat it is. They are not mucking around, these parents."[51]

The University of Technology Sydney's Christina Ho found in her research that "some families believe entry into a selective school will secure their child's future".[52] The myth of parental choice inevitably drives this kind of anxiety, especially as parents feel increasingly judged for their choice of school. And, as any decent marketer can tell you, choice itself drives anxiety. Ho points to children studying for 18 months before the supposedly all-important entrance tests, including lucrative scholarship exams for entry into prestigious private schools. Pity the poor child who wins one of those. The relentless pressure to maintain their grades will not let up for six long years. Public selective schools, just like public schools generally, do not have the same freedom to exclude enrolled students.

Ho's article also points to the toll on kids whose parents are so desperate to gain them a foothold on the ruthless neoliberal education ladder:

> This culture of extreme study and competitive schooling raises profound questions about the implications for student wellbeing. Some students spoke about their fatigue. As one student said:

> "I work up to late at night. So sometimes I feel drowsy and I yawn a bit and have water in my eyes."[53]

"Their teachers also expressed concern about insufficient sleep and heightened stress caused by the pressure to get into a selective school," Ho explained.

> They described students' tears if they were not successful when the results came out. One teacher said he had a "blanket rule" of not talking about the tests in the classroom, because his students were so preoccupied with ensuring they were doing enough preparation. Other teachers reflected on students' fear of taking risks because of the culture of perfectionism associated with scoring and ranking through tests.

It is worth remembering that Ho's research is about entrance exams that children take when they are 9, 10 or 11 years old. The effect of all this pressure and competition is damaging.

According to the Australian Institute of

Health and Welfare, mental health disorders among young people have risen by almost 50% over the last 15 years, with anxiety rising at the fastest rate.[54] Anxiety is the inevitable result of neoliberalism's zero-sum view of the world. It is this that drives the belief that for your kid to get ahead they must climb over other kids. And for them to do that, you as their parent must make the right choice.

Human beings don't like no choice, but they don't like unlimited choice either.[55] Too much choice creates a fear about which choice is the right one. See super funds and rooftop solar, if you doubt me. Given the weight that we now put on choosing the mythical "right" school for our children, school choice has made many parents feel like shit.

It works like this. If you choose one school you must decide to reject the rest. How do you know, in advance, if you've chosen wisely? One way is to buy the most expensive school you can afford, because capitalism has convinced us that a higher price means better quality. Feeling you must buy a fancy school (or the fanciest you can manage) to prove you are a good parent increases stress and anxiety in another way. It leads to families spending money they don't have.

Successive governments have convinced parents that they must pay for their kids' education. We are even grooming young parents via the outrageous childcare fees charged by that largely privatised industry. Childcare can easily cost as much as sending a kid to an expensive private primary or secondary school. We have convinced at least a couple of generations of parents that they must pay through the nose for something that most of their grandparents got for nothing. This has added to the running-hard-to-stay-in-the-same-place lifestyle so many young families are struggling with today. HECS debts, impossibly high house prices and exorbitant private school fees are leaching the joy out of family life. No wonder exhaustion and anxiety levels are skyrocketing.

The drive to find the "right" school for your child leads to kids being ferried all over capital cities on long commutes. And if you have more than one child and have swallowed the "right" school idea holus-bolus, it can lead to multiple trips every morning and afternoon. This adds to stress and time pressure, and not just for parents and kids either. Witness the huge relief everyone feels in school holidays as the traffic jams of term time disappear. And I have not even mentioned the environmental impacts of all that driving around.

—

Over the last half century, we have created a system of publicly funded schools, both public and private, that is unique in the world. Although, to be fair, the Heritage Foundation beloved of Donald Trump and his cronies seems to have taken inspiration from it.[56] We have given the chronically underfunded public system all the responsibilities and expect it to accept every child, including the most disadvantaged and so most expensive to teach, while starving it of resources. We have given sometimes extravagantly overfunded private schools all the rights, including the right to isolate themselves from the toughest end of education. As a result, we now have one of the most segregated education systems in the OECD, and we are continuing to use public funding to increase that segregation which is currently rising at the second fastest rate.[57]

For those kids in the so-called "good" schools,

results have at best flatlined. For those in what are rapidly becoming residualised schools, results have plummeted. And we haven't just segregated our kids along class lines. We have sliced and diced them every way we can think of. We put girls with girls, boys with boys (though, as I've suggested above, that might be changing a little), smart kids with smart kids, rich kids with rich kids, poor kids with poor kids, Christian kids with Christian kids, Muslim kids with Muslim kids, Jewish kids with Jewish kids, Catholic kids with ... oh, wait ... I'm not so sure most kids in Catholic schools are very Catholic anymore, sporty kids with sporty kids, arty kids with arty kids, black kids with black kids and white kids with white kids. Is this a good idea? Will it build a cohesive society? Does it help our kids to get to know one another and help break down prejudice? Or does it do the opposite?

Segregation by social class has all sorts of perverse consequences. We have seen the development of a particularly nauseating kind of social tourism where richer, predominantly private school kids are sent overseas to build orphanages and perform other charitable services in developing countries to "broaden their horizons". They call it "international service". The trouble is, it's occasionally been a scam, causing more harm than good.

In 2018, Australia became the first country in the world to recognise "orphanage trafficking". It was estimated that 80% of kids in so-called orphanages in countries such as Nepal and Cambodia had at least one parent living and that they were being used to attract wealthy first-worlders looking to assuage their guilt or — see above — broaden their own privileged and protected kids' horizons.[58] If we wanted them to have broader horizons we should just have let them go to school with all the kids in their local area, like most of my peers and I did prior to the 1980s.

## Defending the current system

I keep wondering what exactly the decades of parental choice, neoliberal, competition-driven education policies have gained Australia. Results have not improved. They have fallen. Fees have not become more affordable, particularly at the so called "elite" schools, and as high fees have increased financial hardship, so choice has increased anxiety and stress. And if we think it's bad now, one expert has calculated that on the current trajectory, some private schools may be charging fees of $100,000 a year by 2036.[59]

I have asked defenders of the public funding of private schools why they support our current system, even debated them on the odd occasion. Rarely do they claim anything that adds to the public good. They never cite improvements in either excellence or equity. Instead, I always receive the same answers. It's always more about their right to get the taxpayer to subsidise their private and positional choices than anything else. As I wrote in 2022, let's debunk those justifications one by one.[60]

The most common justification is that private school parents pay taxes, so their child is entitled to be subsidised. Their child is subsidised, like any other child via their entitlement to a fully publicly funded place in their local public school. Even better, this entitlement continues whether they choose to access the place or not. If they should lose their capacity to pay private school fees, their child is unhappy at the private school, or the private school is unhappy with their child, the local public school will accept them, no questions asked.

The same is not true in reverse.

The fact that a family decides not to take up their public school place is not a justification for the funding to transfer to a different school. Taxation is not a deposit account that we can draw on to "buy" whatever service we choose. Childless taxpayers also fund schools. According to the taxpayer argument, they should be able to withdraw that money.

Our taxes fund public transport but just because someone chooses not to catch a train or a bus, we don't believe their choice of private car should be subsidised by the taxpayer. Yet, car drivers could make many of the same arguments that private school supporters do. After all, by choosing not to use public transport they could argue they leave more space for other commuters. Or that if everyone used public transport, the system would be overwhelmed.

But it is worse than that. Given that public schools educate the vast majority of our most disadvantaged children, those who argue that fee-charging schools should be subsidised to support their choice are essentially saying that families who have no choice should subsidise those who do. And subsidise them to buy what they perceive is an educational advantage: a private and positional good. It is literally a case of the poor subsidising the rich so the better off can shut out the children of the poor and lock them into underfunded schools.

Another common justification is that sending a child to a private school helps public schools by reducing the burden of compulsory education. In fact, as I have argued more than once, the opposite is true. Because when private schools (with a handful of honourable exceptions) carefully choose where they will and will not open campuses and which kids they will or will not educate, all they do is remove many of the most advantaged kids from the public system. In doing this, they actively harm public education.

Fewer kids from wealthy and middle-class backgrounds reduce a public school's ability to fundraise (while increasing its need to do so) and reduce the number of well-educated parents who can advocate and lobby on behalf of their own children's schools and public schools in general. Increasing proportions of students from lower socio-economic backgrounds also reduce the number of parents who can pay even voluntary contributions or elective fees. This can affect the number of courses disadvantaged public schools can afford to offer, further limiting opportunities for needy kids.

By removing the students requiring less support, private schools reduce the economy of scale in public schools. In other words, every middle-class kid who leaves the public system increases the ratio of needier students, thereby increasing the per-student cost. If most kids went to public schools, education would be cheaper for everyone, including governments, and much fairer.

Some people argue that public funding of private schools saves governments money. Putting aside whether the aim of an education system should be to save public money, especially at the expense of the educational opportunities of our neediest kids, that is no longer true, if it ever was. In 2024, research by the Australian Education Union revealed that over half of Australia's private schools now receive more combined government funding per student, from both the federal and state governments, than similar public schools.[61]

Remember when I said our system was arse about? I rest my case.

As I mentioned at the beginning of this essay, in 1962 at the tail end of the baby boom, the Bishop of Goulburn closed the local Catholic schools and told the students to lob up to local public schools. This flamboyant and newsworthy gesture is the source of the myth that the public system would collapse if required to educate all Australian children. Given today's falling birth rate this is no longer relevant, if it ever was. After all, the public system didn't even collapse then.

The rest of the world — including much higher achieving systems than ours — manages to enrol the majority of kids in public schools perfectly well. In fact, it is far more efficient and less wasteful. As it is, we spend too much money on infrastructure due to our parallel systems and not enough on what goes on inside classrooms (and indoor aquatic centres). Besides, I am not suggesting getting rid of private schools entirely, just that we need to redress the extreme bias that burdens public schools and buoys private ones.

Another misconception is that private schools employ the best teachers and get better results. This view is turbocharged by the press and by the ingrained belief that things you pay for must be better than things you don't. However, all teachers have been trained at the same institutions, and many of them move between the public and private systems. Some parents talk about the number of public school teachers who send their children to private schools. What is rarely mentioned is the number of private school teachers who send their kids public, despite the often generous fee subsidies they could claim.

In New South Wales, the Department of Education targets the highest performing education degree graduates and offers them permanent positions in public schools. This is highly sought after and competitive. Those teachers tend to spend a lifetime in the public system. And public schools select teachers on merit, unlike some religious schools who are fighting hard to retain the right to hire teachers who conform to the right religious, moral and social beliefs, with merit a secondary concern.

However, as was recently reported, remote and disadvantaged schools are suffering a chronic teacher shortage, which also results in the number of courses they can offer shrinking.[62] This is not helped by the fact that other publicly funded schools — aka private, fee-charging ones — can and do poach teachers from the public system. In other words, we are funding already advantaged schools to plunder staff from disadvantaged ones.

No wonder there remains a deeply held assumption that private schools do better academically than public schools but, according to research, that is also not true.[63] Once school results are adjusted for the differences in the socio-economic status of the students they enrol, there is no difference in academic results. In fact, from a cost/benefit perspective, it is arguable that public schools do better, given they achieve the same results while spending far less public (and private) money.

Then there is the consistent evidence showing that public school students do better at university than their private school counterparts with the same ATAR.[64] More private school kids get to university, unsurprisingly given the money spent on them and that they are overwhelmingly from higher socio-economic backgrounds, but public school graduates do better once they are there. Maybe it's just easier to go from one underfunded public institution to another underfunded public institution. Some of those kids from the high-fee schools must get the shock of their life as they sit on the stairs in overcrowded lectures and tutorials, wondering where all the luxury has gone.[65]

Another justification I regularly hear concerns the "sacrifices" private school parents make to send their child to an expensive school. This one, I think, is the basis of the "good parents choose private, bad parents choose public" shibboleth. No parent should feel they need to make "sacrifices" to get their child a decent education in the fourth richest country in the world. If that is true, we should all take to the streets. Moreover, deciding to buy your child what you perceive as an advantage cannot be called a "sacrifice". It is nothing more than a purchasing decision, a bit like saying, "I made sacrifices to buy this luxurious house in a prestigious suburb, so I should get a government subsidy."

Other defenders are quick to point out that the public system is stratified too. This is correct. There are no completely equal education systems anywhere in the world. The inevitable differences visited upon each of us at birth have an effect, no matter what. However, that is no argument for taking education funding and, instead of using it to narrow the gaps, using it to widen the inequality even further.

Finally, there is the argument that public funding puts downward pressure on fees. There is precisely no evidence that this has occurred, rather the opposite. Meanwhile, the proportion of disadvantaged students attending independent schools has shrunk dramatically. Hence the alarming synchronicity of 28.9% of students in private schools being from the highest socio-economic backgrounds while exactly 28.9% of the enrolments in public schools come from the lowest.[66] Mirror, mirror on the wall, who has the unfairest education system of them all? How is it reasonable that one publicly subsidised child gets access to an air conditioned equestrian centre, while another must book hourly access to a computer weeks in advance?

Making parents feel that they should, by whatever means, send their kids to a private school has been fuelled by conservative governments who would be happy to send as many families as possible into the private sector, leaving a residual public system for the poor. Not only is it privatisation by stealth, but it also destroys some of the most precious aspects of public education:

ensuring the highest quality education for every child who walks through the gates; and building cohesion and connection within each local community and our nation as a whole.

We will soon be running a Royal Commission into antisemitism and social cohesion. Will it take a peek at our increasingly segregated school system, I wonder? Or does it remain the problem that must not be named?

In summary, most of the benefits of private education are cosmetic: more about buying status than accessing a better education. The tragedy is that Australia is one of the few countries in the world that not only publicly funds the fears, insecurities and status anxieties of some parents but also — just by doing so — actually increases that anxiety. This has been helpful to no one, least of all our children.

# How do we get out of the mess we have made?

Many people, especially educators and education experts, are deeply concerned about where our school system is headed, particularly as it becomes increasingly segregated and divided along class lines. Whatever other sorts of progress we may pride ourselves on, we continue to ignore this most glaring inequality. In their book, *The Privileged Few*, Clive and Myra Hamilton put it like this, "… in contrast to sharp improvements in gender diversity and probably racial diversity, 'class diversity' has deteriorated".[67]

While I am delighted about the strides women have made, I worry that private schooling has somehow colluded with middle-class feminism, albeit unconsciously. As a result of an incomplete feminist revolution, mothers, particularly middle-class mothers, can still feel guilty about using their talents and education — often an expensive private education — to earn money and progress in a career. Private schools offer them a perfect way to soothe their unease. They can claim that they are only going out to work to help pay the school fees, thereby reclaiming their status as good mothers. Given the constant rise in school fees and house prices, for most people, a two-income household is a necessity to cover costs.

As for the gains for people of colour, we have seen decreasing racial diversity in our schools. Our impulse to put like with like is the culprit. Privileged schools do a lot of window dressing to convince us of their "diversity", but the stats tell a different story. According to ACOSS, "public schools educate two-thirds of all Australian students including 80% of children from families of low socio-economic advantage, more than 80% of Aboriginal and Torres Strait Islander children, more than two-thirds of children with a disability and more than 67% of students whose families speak a language other than English at home".[68] The percentage of Indigenous children who attend public schools, for example, is not affected much by tokenistic scholarships or programs that aim to scoop up a handful of high-performing Aboriginal kids and whisk them off to private schools.

To return to my crucial point, this is why the OECD has been repeatedly warning us about just how socially segregated our schools have become and just how rapidly that divide is increasing. Yet most Australians seem either indifferent or blind to what has happened. If they can isolate their own child, they don't seem to care. Worse, many of those who benefit seem to prefer things just the way they are. Hamilton and Hamilton make the point again:

> While social movements demanding women's equality, racial equality and gay rights have made significant progress since the 1970s, demands for more equality in wealth and power have fallen on stony ground. Elite privilege has gone from strength to strength so that the "exclusive elite" … while less male and less white, remains an oligarchy … dominated by the products of the nation's expensive private schools … The most

> obvious harm from this rule by a few is that many talented people not from privileged backgrounds are relegated to lesser positions.[69]

We may not be prepared to admit we have a private-school-led oligarchy, but we know it's there. It's one of the main reasons so many parents scrabble to get their kids into the private system. And the competition I have described in schooling suits the oligarchs. Better we fight one another than them.

It is common to see "exclusive and elite" schools trot out the lucky few they pluck from disadvantaged communities as proof that they do not discriminate. But choosing to promote a few winners from among those you see as losers is not proof of equality. The fact that a few exceptional children from lower socio-economic backgrounds find their way past the many barriers we place in front of them is not an excuse to keep maintaining those barriers or, worse, increasing their size. And our fatally biased education system is not just a disaster for disadvantaged kids. It's a tax on us all. As Hamilton and Hamilton point out, our system has little to do with merit. The mediocre middle class get promoted past their value, while many of the talented from less fortunate backgrounds get left out.

So how do we wind back the damage we have done? Particularly as so few people want to recognise it even exists? I think that Australia is as blind to the damage we are doing to our nation via the social segregation of our schools as America is to the horrific toll their refusal to implement sensible gun controls takes on their society. It is happening for the same reason. Those who feel that their power and influence will be reduced if Australia changes the way it funds schools, or if America controls the numbers and types of weapons its citizens can own, are working very hard to muddy the debates and stop us seeing. Tragically, those who suffer most in both instances are our children.

# The solutions we need

There are solutions. Indeed, the Gonski review was an attempt to make our system fairer, and its recommendations might have had a positive effect, if politics and vested interests had not got involved. Those who care about public education, both as a principle and as an indispensable part of our democracy, must be prepared for the powerful and the privileged to do all they can to head off any changes. Therefore, as I consider potential solutions, I will examine how politically possible they may be, as well as how effective.

The first suggestion about making our schooling systems more equal is, I believe, also the most politically achievable. It is something that has been suggested by many people, including participants in a national symposium on funding, equity and achievement in Australian schools, all of whom believe that all schools in receipt of public money be subject to the same obligations.[70] In other words, all publicly funded schools should have to abide by the same standards of compliance, implementation and accountability for enrolment, behaviour and inclusion. This seems reasonable and logical, especially as many private schools now receive as much, if not more, public funding per student than the similar public school down the road.[71]

In practice this would mean that private schools, once they had enrolled a student, would not be able to exclude that student for any reason that differs from the standard required from a public school to do the same. Perhaps even exclusion because of the nonpayment of fees should be subject to negotiation and arbitration by a body such as the Department of Education. This would stop the children private schools decide they don't want from being dumped on the already underfunded nearby public school, thereby compounding their degree of difficulty. It would also require publicly funded private schools shoulder at least some of the responsibility for compulsory education. As such, it is an eminently arguable proposition. Why should some schools in receipt of public funding have obligations to the public good, while other schools have none?

The current education funding reforms, meant to bring every school up to its SRS (School Resource Standard), will not kick in fully until 2034. Worse, they may still not be fully funded even then, given the definition of "fully funded" is disputed. And public schools will have to jump through various performance and attendance hoops to get their money. As I mentioned, all private schools must do in return for their public funding is obey the law and teach the curriculum. They don't even have to follow the full requirements of anti-discrimination legislation. The double standard is stark.

Education researchers Tom Greenwell and Chris Bonnor in their book, *Waiting for Gonski*, take this idea a step further. They suggest that all schools should be offered the chance of being totally publicly funded as long as they agree not to charge fees. They could keep their "special" character, usually religious, but would have to accept all children who wanted to attend within their area.[72] As they would if the symposium's reforms were implemented, some private schools, especially high-fee ones, might decide this was a bridge too far and decline the offer. In which case they would lose their public funding and be self-supporting. This would then release some badly needed dollars for schools struggling with high concentrations of disadvantage.

Greenwell and Bonnor call this "The Ontario Solution" as that's what schools in the Canadian province have done. Chris Bonnor told me about the shock the Catholic bishops of Ontario expressed when it was suggested that their schools could charge fees. They saw it as utterly antithetical to their religious mission. Maybe they should come and have a chat with the Catholic bishops in this country.

In both the United Kingdom and New Zealand, the majority of religious schools are part of the public system. They do not charge fees, must accept all local kids who want to come, but may keep their religious character. The only problem with this suggestion is that the private schools will fight it to the death and that matters because they are exceptionally powerful lobbyists. They can have their cake and eat it now. Mind you, they will probably fight to the death against any attempt to rebalance the scales.

The symposium I mentioned was run in 2023 by the education faculty at the University of Melbourne.[73] It was tasked with making suggestions about what could be done to stop Australia slipping deeper into the low equity, low achievement OECD quadrant. I was one of the presenters. Below are some further suggestions that were made.

## Implement the Gonski recommendation for School Planning Authorities in every jurisdiction

This would stop new schools being opened willy-nilly and cannibalising other publicly funded schools nearby. Only open new schools where there is a need for one, in other words. The former NSW education minister Verity Firth in her speech to the symposium asked a pertinent question:

> Australian governments fund non-government schools to set up in local areas in direct competition with government schools. They fund multiple schools in

> a geographic location, all of whom are competing with each other for students, leaving some students with no choice but the school with the fewest students and the least resources. Is there any other area of public policy where the government funds its competitor and in so doing, reduces its own institutions' capacity to perform and makes the task of performance more expensive?[74]

In 2025, the NSW government pledged to build 100 new preschools in public schools by 2027, just for a moment giving its own schools a competitive advantage. By the end of the year, however, it also committed to giving $60 million to build them in some private schools as well.[75] Sigh. As Firth says, where else do we expect governments to fund their own services and then insist they also fund their competition in the name of (ahem) "fairness"?

## Acknowledge the unique role public schools bear in shouldering the responsibility for compulsory education

Take the weight public schools carry into account in funding and regulatory decisions. For example, I have heard parents complain bitterly that they do not know what class their child will be in at a public school in advance, and sometimes not for days after the school year has started. This is due to public schools never being sure how many children will turn up expecting to be enrolled.

Private schools do not have this issue. Yet the uncertainty is caused by our weird hybrid system.

Public schools in other countries are better able to calculate future enrolments based on demographics than Australia, which adds to cost, confusion and the duplication of administration. The symposium recommended that schools that experience greater fluctuations in enrolments — up or down — than the total change in an area should receive additional funding, and those that experience more stable enrolments should receive less funding. Schools that accept kids who have been excluded from other schools should receive extra funding, while the excluding schools should lose the same amount.

The symposium was also concerned about the disproportionate number of early career teachers in public schools, especially disadvantaged schools. It recommended that those schools receive additional funding for professional development and support to help make sure that our most vulnerable kids don't miss out on high quality teachers. It strikes me that such an investment might also help stem the departure of teachers, highest in the first five years, who resign due to feeling overwhelmed and burnt out. Nothing destroys a teacher's morale faster than knowing what would help a struggling child while being denied the resources they need to be able to offer it.

Further to this, although also not suggested at the symposium, is another question. Should overfunded private schools (and that's almost all of them according to SRS) be able to poach teachers from underfunded (that's also almost all of them) disadvantaged public schools, especially hard to staff schools, with offers of higher salaries and other perks? Should the government be funding schools to remove teachers from those classrooms where they are most desperately needed?

Private schools do not have to reveal what they pay their principals, despite their public funding, but the recent leaking of a salary benchmarking report indicated that in 2021 they were receiving between $460,000 and $1,034,000 a year. As Julie Hare's 2025 article pointed out, salaries are likely to have increased since then.[76] The same article puts public school principals' salaries — with a vastly tougher job to do — at between $200,000 and $250,000.

## Reconsider private school tax exemptions

Review the transparency and fairness of things like tax expenditures and foregone revenues and reconsider the charitable status of private schools, especially those charging high fees. Because Australian private schools, almost alone in the world, can be public when it comes to the handing out of public money but private when it comes to indirect funding such as tax exemptions and charitable donations, such sources of revenue should be investigated, made public and calculated as part of the per-student public funding private schools receive. State governments should not give tax advantages to private schools and private schools should not be exempt from paying local government rates. Especially as they rarely contribute much to their local government area, except high demand for parking and sometimes predatory absorption of local land and buildings.

It is also worth remembering that virtually all private schools qualify as charities, whereas public schools — because they are seen as an arm of government — do not. That is why the Public Education Foundation was founded — to enable people to make tax deductible donations to public schools.

There are other suggestions, including having a sliding scale of subsidy depending on fees charged. After all, if a private school charges more in fees alone than the average cost of educating a child in a public school — that enrols a much higher proportion of expensive to teach kids — why should they receive a public subsidy on top? This is really a way to cap the fees private schools can charge in return for the government subsidy they receive. Such a move might actually make such schools more affordable.

These are all eminently sensible and reasonable suggestions that might help restore some semblance of equality of opportunity between our two systems. Of course, if I could wave a magic wand, I would go back to the way things were in 1963, when I first arrived in this country. Back then we gave public money to public schools and private schools relied on private money. It was simple, logical and efficient. The mess we have now fails on all those fronts. However, magic wands being scarce on the ground, if all the above falls on deaf ears, and it well might given the forces arraigned against public education in Australia, I have another suggestion.

If we are really going to decide that many public schools in Australia are to become welfare schools of last resort for the poor, although I sincerely hope that we do not, then we need to start funding them that way.

We must shatter the illusion that there is anything remotely fair or equitable about the way we featherbed the schools that overwhelmingly educate the advantaged and deliberately hobble the schools that are left to deal with the poor. If we are going to turn our schools into ghettos of privilege and underprivilege, and given our world-beating segregation by social class, we are already well on the way, then we must fund the schools with concentrations of disadvantage up the wazoo. We must fund them and resource them as the welfare hubs that they will need to become.

To get the schools that such a rich country deserves, we need to take the following steps.

1. Reduce class sizes in the schools enrolling the most disadvantaged to a maximum of 10 to 15 students and provide those children with not just a superb, well-paid class teacher but with learning support teachers, remedial support specialists, speech therapists, counsellors, nurses, welfare, social and youth workers as well. Children who do not feel safe cannot learn.

2. Give the teachers at these schools lots of relief from face-to-face teaching so they can continuously plan lessons for their very needy students. Pay them a premium

for the degree of difficulty they face in their classrooms. Exhausted teachers cannot teach.

3. Provide not just breakfasts but nutritious and free lunches and free fruit, vegetables and milk throughout the school day. Hungry children cannot learn.

4. Test every child's eyesight and give them free glasses if required. Children who cannot see the electronic whiteboard cannot learn.

5. Equip disadvantaged school libraries with every latest technological educational aid and as many exciting, colourful and entertaining books as there is space for them. The digital divide is real, but so is the book divide.

6. Ensure classrooms are clean, comfortable, well-lit and both warm in winter and cool in summer. Crumbling classrooms and buildings send a derisory message to both students and staff. Children who are too

hot or too cold cannot learn. Teachers who are too hot or too cold cannot teach.

7. Provide all vaccinations, dental care and medications as part of the school's budget. As one teacher said to me, if you want to know how disadvantaged a school is, don't look at their ICSEA (Index of Community Socio-Educational Advantage), look at their teeth.

8. If we realistically expect to change their life trajectories, support the children born into disadvantage long before they reach school. We know who the women are who are likely to have such children. We need to support those women from the moment they get pregnant with proper prenatal care, secure housing, proper food and nutrition, treatment for mental health issues and addiction problems, parenting classes, and help with literacy and numeracy. Once the baby is born, postnatal care should include weekly visits by a baby healthcare nurse, continued parenting training and literacy

> and numeracy, job readiness training, plus — as soon as the child is able — first-class early childhood education at well-funded, free, public childcare centres. All this would mean that far fewer children, unlucky in the lottery of birth, would be behind the educational eight ball before they ever go to school.

If we did all of this, and we could afford to given the savings it would make in the lifetime cost of our most disadvantaged children — in crime reduction, mental health, homelessness and addiction alone — we could make a real difference.

We still attach shame to poverty and lower social class. Going to a public school is becoming stigmatised in Australia. Parents who actively choose a public school for their children are routinely and sometimes rudely required to defend their choice. This conflict between parents is, sadly, exactly what you can expect if you use your education system to build a class system.

Every day we tell our neediest kids — and their families and communities — that they are worthless. If we funded our disadvantaged schools the ways I suggest we would send the opposite message. Indeed, they would stop being disadvantaged schools and become merely the schools that were dedicated to educating disadvantaged children. This is something we both could and should do if we wish to be thought of as a civilised country. If we want to be the clever country, creating world-leading artists, scientists, thinkers and creatives of all kinds, we must educate all our potential talent. The fact that most of the rest of the world more equitably educates its children puts us all at a competitive disadvantage, no matter where we went to school.

If that wasn't bad enough, increasingly seeing schooling as a private and positional good, rather than a public one, has not even benefited those who have chosen fee-charging schools. In fact, according to recent research by The Australia Institute, Australia now has the most expensive high schools system in the world.[77] It costs parents an average of $4,967 for every year of high school for every child. That's *four times* the average price that parents in other OECD countries pay.

But, as the authors of the paper point out, "despite this high level of private spending, the educational performance of the Australian high school system is falling".[78] This high cost, according to researchers Skye Predavec and Richard Denniss, is directly caused by our weird hybrid system of publicly subsidised public and private schools. "Australians spend more on high school education per student than in any other developed country. This is because of Australia's unusually high rate of private schooling and very high private school fees."[79]

It seems as if our neoliberal governments from the last two decades — both Labor and Coalition (since they all drank the Kool-Aid) — have stealthily and successfully transferred the cost of educating Australia's children to their parents. This has not just decimated the opportunities of children whose parents can't afford to pay, it has had devastating results for all our children and their families, no matter where they live or how much they earn. Not only has their education, luxuriously presented or otherwise, become inferior, but they have lost contact and connection with one another. Let's hope that was an unintended consequence; but given the threat democracy appears to be under globally right now, in my more cynical moments, I cannot help wondering whether divide and conquer was the plan all along.

The ideal of a strong public education system

funded by everyone, for the benefit of everyone, originally developed alongside the ideal of representative democracy, which is a parliament selected by everyone, for the benefit of everyone. Democracy for all requires education for all. The two are indivisible. They are both products of the same essential moral value; namely that all human beings are created equal and should have as equal as possible rights to learn and develop, not just as workers, but as citizens and human beings. Neoliberalism divides the world into winners and losers, lifters and leaners; those who "deserve" to get ahead and those who do not. Its bedrock lack of generosity has cost us all dearly.

My mother was right. A strong, well-resourced public education system, supported by all but a privileged few (and more fool them) is the mark of a civilised, well-organised nation working to respect, protect and enhance the lives of all its citizens. Unfortunately, we are throwing it away with both hands. Public schools are an expression of a public good: the common good. They are hanging by a thread. We jettison them at our peril.

# Endnotes

1 Wright (2025) "Private school fees and luxury cars driving surge in bankruptcies", https://www.smh.com.au/politics/federal/private-school-fees-and-luxury-cars-driving-surge-in-bankruptcies-20251211-p5nmqc.html
2 Parliament of Australia (no date) "Chapter 1 — Schools funding: a historical and political context", https://www.aph.gov.au/Parliamentary_Business/Committees/Senate/Education_Employment_and_Workplace_Relations/Completed_inquiries/2002-04/schoolfunding/report/03ch1
3 Stark and Finke (2000) "Catholic religious vocations: decline and revival", https://www.baylorisr.org/wp-content/uploads/stark_vocations.pdf
4 Bourke (2018) "Catholic Church national wealth estimated to be $30 billion, investigation finds", https://www.abc.net.au/news/2018-02-13/catholic-church-worth-$30-billion-investigation-finds/9422246
5 Fraser and Simons (2015) *Malcolm Fraser: The Political Memoirs*, Miegunyah Press, p 175
6 Connors and McMorrow (2015) "Imperatives in Schools Funding: Equity, sustainability and achievement", Australian Council for Educational Research
7 Lee (2020) "The dog fight over school funding that went all the way to the High Court", https://www.abc.net.au/news/2020-05-12/

the-history-listen-the-forgotten-fight-over-school-funding-dogs/12101774

8 Knight writing on Lowe (1967) *Australian Dictionary of Biography*, https://adb.anu.edu.au/biography/lowe-robert-2376

9 Chaudhry (2022) "How higher literacy rates can fight poverty", https://borgenproject.org/literacy-rates/

10 Cranston et al (2010) "Politics and school education in Australia: a case of shifting purposes", *Journal of Educational Administration*, 48(2), pp 182–195, https://eprints.qut.edu.au/44173/

11 Duffy (2025) "Education leaders call on News Corp to cease 'harmful' NAPLAN league tables", https://www.abc.net.au/news/2025-12-05/news-corp-naplan-league-tables-education-leaders-open-letter/106100742

12 Predavec and Denniss (2026) "Australia's private high school problem: unequal, expensive, and falling behind", https://australiainstitute.org.au/report/australias-private-high-school-problem/

13 Hare (2024) "The cost of sending your child to a private school — in seven charts", https://www.afr.com/work-and-careers/education/the-cost-of-sending-your-child-to-a-private-school-in-seven-charts-20240131-p5f1cc

14 Cranston et al (2010)

15 ABC (2004) "PM's private school stance a disgrace: unions", https://www.abc.net.au/news/2004-01-20/pms-private-school-stance-a-disgrace-unions/122534

16 *The Age* (2005) "Values emblem a bit of an ass", https://www.theage.com.au/national/values-emblem-a-bit-of-an-ass-20050826-ge0rf7.html

17 Cobbold (2010) "A Critique of the SES Funding Model for Private Schools", https://saveourschools.com.au/funding/a-critique-of-the-ses-funding-model-for-private-schools/

18 Parliament of Australia (2002) National School Chaplaincy Program media release, https://parlinfo.aph.gov.au/parlInfo/search/display/display.w3p;query=Id:%22media/pressrel/D7MV6%22

19 Eacott (2024) "The effect of abolishing the New Schools Policy on the provision of schools and enrolments in Australia", *Journal of Educational Administration and History Issue 3*, p. 252, https://www.tandfonline.com/doi/full/10.1080/00220620.2024.2353020

20 The Heritage Foundation (2023) *Mandate for Leadership: the Conservative Promise*, https://static.heritage.org/project2025/2025_MandateForLeadership_FULL.pdf

21 Sharma (2025) "Rethinking Education Governance: Insights from Chile's Reform Journey through a Systems Thinking Lens", https://www.hks.harvard.edu/centers/cid/voices/rethinking-education-governance-insights-chiles-reform-journey-through-systems

22 Australian Government (2011) *Review of Funding for Schooling: Final Report, December 2011*, https://www.education.gov.au/school-funding/resources/review-funding-schooling-final-report-december-2011

23 The Office Space (no date) "The changing face of Australian education", https://www.theofficespace.com.au/the-changing-face-of-australias-education-system/#:~:text=The%2520Gonski%2520Report%2520–%2520The%25202011,literacy%252C%2520and%2520thirteenth%2520for%2520maths

24 Aston (2016) "Marginal seat voters back Gonski 2-1: Poll", https://www.smh.com.au/politics/federal/marginal-seat-voters-back-gonski-21-poll-20160206-gmncej.html

25 Baker (2022) "No Gonski 'nirvana': Why Australia's

most ambitious education reforms have failed", https://www.smh.com.au/education/no-gonski-nirvana-why-australia-s-most-ambitious-education-reforms-have-failed-20220215-p59wpj.html

26 De Bortoli (2023) "Australian teenagers record steady results in international tests, but about half are not meeting proficiency standards", https://www.acer.org/my/news/article/australian-teenagers-record-steady-results-in-international-tests-but-about-half-are-not-meeting-proficiency-standards#:~:text=How%20did%20Australia%20go?,Greece%2C%20New%20Zealand%20and%20Sweden.

27 Tillett (2010) "No school to lose funds: Gillard", https://thewest.com.au/news/australia/no-school-to-lose-funds-gillard-ng-ya-215609

28 Australian Education Union (2023) "Research reveals widening resource gaps between public and private schools", https://www.aeufederal.org.au/news-media/media-releases/2023/november/research-reveals-widening-resource-gaps-between-public-and-private-schools

29 Cobbold (2025) "The $30 Billion School Funding Cuts — Fact Check", https://saveourschools.com.au/funding/the-30-billion-school-funding-cuts-fact-check/

30 Department of Education (2025) "Reports on school funding", https://www.education.gov.au/schooling/reports-school-funding

31 McGowan (2018) "Scott Morrison sends his children to private school to avoid 'skin curling' sexuality discussions", https://www.theguardian.com/australia-news/2018/sep/03/scott-morrison-sends-his-children-to-private-school-to-avoid-skin-curling-sexuality-discussions

32 McGowan (2018) "Scott Morrison sends his children to private school to avoid 'skin curling'

sexuality discussions", https://www.theguardian.com/australia-news/2018/sep/03/scott-morrison-sends-his-children-to-private-school-to-avoid-skin-curling-sexuality-discussions

33 Davies (2021) "Private schools reap hundreds of millions of dollars in JobKeeper funding", https://www.theguardian.com/australia-news/2021/jun/29/private-schools-reap-hundreds-of-millions-of-dollars-in-jobkeeper-funding

34 Roddan (2021) "Private schools reap $750m in JobKeeper", https://www.afr.com/politics/federal/private-schools-reap-750m-in-jobkeeper-20211006-p58xlj

35 Caro (2020) "How schools have become political pawns", https://www.thesaturdaypaper.com.au/opinion/topic/2020/05/02/how-schools-have-become-political-pawns/15883416009757

36 Kelly (2021) "Row erupts over air purifiers at NSW schools as parents fear Covid spread", https://www.theguardian.com/australia-news/2021/oct/20/row-erupts-over-air-purifiers-at-nsw-schools-as-parents-fear-covid-spread?CMP=Share_iOSApp_Other

37 Australian Government (2020) *Education in Remote and Complex Environments — Impact of the COVID-19 Pandemic on Home Learning and Teaching*, p. 11

38 Independent Expert Panel's Review to Inform a Better and Fairer Education System (2023), *Improving Outcomes for All: The Report of the Independent Expert Panel's Review to Inform a Better and Fairer Education System*, p. 78, https://www.education.gov.au/download/17515/expert-panels-report/36062/document/pdf

39 Independent Expert Panel's Review to Inform a Better and Fairer Education System (2023), *Improving Outcomes for All: The Report of the Independent Expert Panel's Review to Inform a Better and Fairer Education System*, p. 78

40 Rorris (2023) "How school funding fails public schools. How to change for the better" https://www.aeufederal.org.au/application/files/3817/0018/3742/Rorris_FundingFailsPublicSchools.pdf

41 Smee (2026) "Science teachers from Queensland Open Brethren schools told to teach students about vegetarian dinosaurs on Noah's Ark", https://www.theguardian.com/australia-news/2026/jan/25/science-teachers-from-queensland-open-brethren-schools-told-to-teach-students-about-vegetarian-dinosaurs-on-noahs-ark

42 Badami (2025) correspondence with the author

43 Keddie (2024) "When picking schools, don't get stuck on single-sex versus co-ed", https://redi.deakin.edu.au/2024/12/when-picking-schools-dont-get-stuck-on-single-sex-vs-co-ed-instead-ask-are-all-students-supported-and-included/

44 Wright (2025)

45 Smith (2024) "This Sydney school is full and turning students away — before 3255 new homes are built nearby", https://www.smh.com.au/politics/nsw/this-sydney-school-is-full-and-turning-students-away-before-3255-new-homes-are-built-nearby-20241229-p5l11x.html

46 Carroll and Gladstone (2024) "Revealed: Sydney's most overcrowded primary and high schools", https://www.smh.com.au/national/nsw/revealed-sydney-s-most-overcrowded-primary-and-high-schools-20240501-p5fo8k.html

47 Von Stumm et al (2020) "Predicting educational achievement from genomic measures and socioeconomic status", https://pubmed.ncbi.nlm.nih.gov/31758750/#:~:text=Abstract,low%20SES%20backgrounds%20attend%20university

48 Barcley Consulting (2024) "The Gold Coast

Schoolyard: A Crossroads of Gender Equity", https://barcley.com.au/gender-equity-gold-coast-schools/

49 Tarek Goodwin (2025) "Chaos erupts at sites of selective school exams as riot squad called to control crowds", https://www.abc.net.au/news/2025-05-02/nsw-riot-squad-called-control-chaos-selective-school-exam-sites/105245958

50 Kowal and Carroll (2025) "'They are not mucking around, these parents': Scale of selective test chaos emerges", https://www.smh.com.au/national/nsw/they-are-not-mucking-around-these-parents-scale-of-selective-test-chaos-emerges-20250507-p5lx7q.html

51 Kowal and Carroll (2025)

52 Ho (2025) "'No pain, no gain': why some primary students are following intense study routines", https://theconversation.com/no-pain-no-gain-why-some-primary-students-are-following-intense-study-routines-256815

53 Ho (2025)

54 Branley and Goloubeva (2023) "Mental health disorders in young Australians surge by 47 per cent over 15 years, new data shows", https://www.abc.net.au/news/2023-10-05/abs-data-shows-mental-health-anxiety-depression-rising/102928618

55 The Decision Lab (no date) "Why do we have a harder time choosing when we have more options?", https://thedecisionlab.com/biases/choice-overload-bias

56 The Heritage Foundation (2023)

57 Varadharajan and Noone (2022) "Australia's education system is one of the most unequal in the OECD. But we know how to help fix it", https://theconversation.com/australias-education-system-is-one-of-the-most-unequal-in-the-oecd-but-we-know-how-to-help-fix-it-177059; Australian Government (2023)

*Improving Outcomes for All*, figure 10, p 78.

58 BBC (2018) "Australia says orphanage trafficking is modern-day slavery", https://www.bbc.com/news/world-australia-46390627.amp

59 Bowes (2026) "Elite private school fees to hit $100,000 a year in a decade", https://www.afr.com/work-and-careers/education/elite-private-school-fees-to-hit-100-000-a-year-in-a-decade-20251119-p5ngra

60 Caro (2022) "Myths about school funding — and how to bust them", https://news.aeuvic.asn.au/in-depth/myths-about-school-funding-and-how-to-bust-them/

61 Australian Education Union (2024) "Majority of private schools get more public funding than comparable public schools", https://www.aeufederal.org.au/news-media/media-releases/2024/september/majority-private-schools-get-more-public-funding-comparable-public-schools

62 Cassidy (2025) "'Diabolical': why Australia's teacher shortages are among the worst in the world — and who is suffering most", https://www.theguardian.com/australia-news/2025/nov/03/australia-teacher-shortage-crisis-regional-disadvantaged-schools?

63 Goss and Emslie (2018) "The expensive truth about private schools and student learning", https://grattan.edu.au/news/here-is-the-expensive-truth-about-private-schools-and-student-learning/#:~:text=Students%20at%20private%20schools%20in,students%20and%20government%20school%20students

64 Preston (2014) "State school kids do better at uni", https://theconversation.com/state-school-kids-do-better-at-uni-29155#:~:text=The%20general%20finding%20is%20that,the%20same%20tertiary%20entrance%20score

65 Harris (2025) "'I had to sit on the floor': Sydney

University adds thousands of extra students", https://www.smh.com.au/national/nsw/i-had-to-sit-on-the-floor-sydney-university-adds-thousands-of-extra-students-20251103-p5n7da.html

66 Independent Expert Panel's Review to Inform a Better and Fairer Education System (2023), *Improving Outcomes for All: The Report of the Independent Expert Panel's Review to Inform a Better and Fairer Education System*, p. 78

67 Hamilton and Hamilton (2024) *The Privileged Few*, Polity, p 108

68 Australian Research Alliance for Children & Youth (2024) "Australia's Children Don't Deserve 10 Years Of Disadvantage — And Australia Can't Afford It", https://www.aracy.org.au/news/australias-children-dont-deserve-10-years-of-disadvantage-and-australia-cant-afford-it/

69 Hamilton and Hamilton (2024)

70 Preston (2023) *Funding, Equity and Achievement in Australian Schools: A report on a national symposium*, https://www.barbaraprestonresearch.com.au/documents/2023_BPreston_Funding_Equity_Achievement_in_Australian_Schools_Symposium_Report.pdf

71 Australian Education Union (2024) "Majority of private schools get more public funding than comparable public schools"

72 Greenwell and Bonnor (2022) *Waiting for Gonski*, UNSW Press

73 Preston (2023) "Funding, Equity and Achievement in Australian Schools", https://www.barbaraprestonresearch.com.au/documents/2023_BPreston_Funding_Equity_Achievement_in_Australian_Schools_Symposium_Report.pdf

74 Preston (2023) "Funding, Equity and Achievement in Australian Schools", p. 17

75 Kowal (2025) "Sydney private schools to receive cash for new preschools", https://www.smh.com.au/politics/nsw/sydney-private-schools-to-receive-cash-for-new-preschools-20251030-p5n6js.html

76 Hare (2025) "Private schools multi-million dollar principals", https://www.thesaturdaypaper.com.au/news/education/2025/12/13/private-schools-million-dollar-principals

77 Predavec and Denniss (2026) "Australia's private high school problem: unequal, expensive, and falling behind", https://australiainstitute.org.au/report/australias-private-high-school-problem/

78 Predavec and Denniss (2026)

79 Predavec and Denniss (2026)

# Acknowledgements

The American writer PJ O'Rourke once said (on *Q&A*, I think) 'beyond a certain point complexity is fraud.' I always remember that when I come to write anything about the complicated, convoluted and idiosyncratic way Australia funds its schools. There are probably only a handful of people who really understand it, which is lovely for those who want to cherry-pick facts and obfuscate how unbelievably unfair it is.

After 25 years as an activist on this subject, I probably understand it better than most punters, but I still need to draw on the wisdom and encyclopaedic knowledge of those who have been studying and fighting in this space even longer than I have. Especially for an essay as comprehensive as this one.

The brains trust I have unashamedly exploited is truly remarkable. They range from academics and ex principals to retired senior bureaucrats, policy advisors, economists, activists and researchers. They include Lyndsay Connors, Dr Jim McMorrow, Dr Helen Proctor, Chris Bonnor, Barbara Preston, Professor Jane Kenway, Ann Caro, Sunil Badami and Jim Watterston. I have also drawn heavily on the work of Adam Rorris, Trevor Cobbold, Richard Dennis, Skye Predavec, Christina Ho, Tom Greenwell and Clive and Myra Hamilton.

There are many others who have taught me much about our schooling system and the bizarre way we fund it, too numerous to mention. Suffice to say they include every teacher, principal and passionate supporter of free, universal, secular public education, open to all, paid for by all, that I have ever met.

Finally thanks are also due to The Australia Institute for asking me to write this essay and Vantage Point's indefatigable editors Alice Grundy and Rod Morrison who kindly but firmly helped me knock this into shape.

## About The Australia Institute

The Australia Institute conducts research that drives the public debate and secures policy outcomes to make Australia better.

The Australia Institute's independence and nonpartisanship ensure our work is guided by a vision for a fairer Australia, without political or commercial influence. Our research regularly calls into question powerful vested interests, multinational corporations, and the economic orthodoxy.

This work is only possible because of independent donations. The support of our donors powers the Institute's ability to fulfil its motto: research that matters. To contribute to our work and ongoing research, you can make a donation on our website by scanning the QR code below.

DOLLARS & SENSE

with Greg Jericho

The Australia Institute
Research that matters

# Become a subscriber

- Receive four thought-provoking essays from leading experts each year
- Short enough to read in one or two sittings, long enough for in-depth analysis
- Free postage within Australia

Australia Institute Press

## Vantage Point Issue 5

Read it and pass it on. Put your name and email below and start a conversation with other readers.

| Name | Contact |
| --- | --- |
| | |
| | |
| | |
| | |
| | |
| | |
| | |